For Stellan,
who inspires me endlessly in the funniest ways.

For Amanda,
whose undying support moves me to achieve great things.

My Funny Body
First Published in 2010 by Bulletproof Toddler
Copyright © 2010 Matthew Swanlund
All Rights Reserved

Requests for permission should be directed to myfunnybody@gmail.com.

ISBN-13: 978-0615425078 (Bulletproof Toddler)

ISBN-10: 0615425070

Library of Congress Cataloging-in-Publication Data Pending

Printed in the United States of America

First Edition

My Funny Body

BY MATTHEW SWANLUND

A BULLETPROOF TODDLER PUBLICATION

My body is really funny.
New things every day.
Sometimes gross or scary,
but everything is okay.

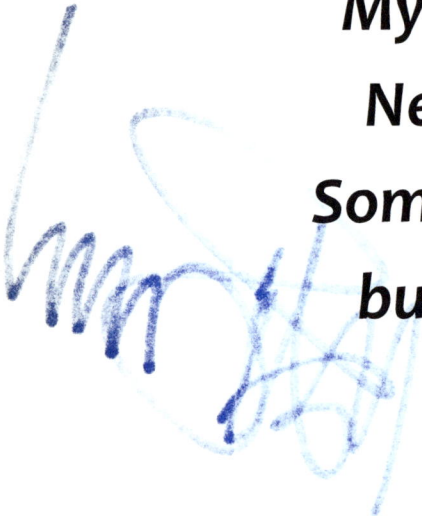

All of it is normal,
even though I sometimes shout!
Fluids, solids and gasses,
are always coming out.

I SNEEZE a lot in Springtime,
because of the flowers and leaves.
No reason to be afraid though,
even if it shakes the trees.

I have EYE BOOGERS every morning,
but I know that they're normal.
I wipe them off before I eat.
I wouldn't want them in my cereal.

Whenever I catch a cold,
SNOT runs out my nose.
Sometimes there's a lot of snot,
so I keep a tissue close.

I cut my knee and BLOOD came out.

I was afraid it wouldn't stop.

But it stopped bleeding on its own,

and Mom put a bandage on top.

Sometimes I just have to BURP,
to let out all the air bubbles.
Trying to burp as loud as I can,
usually gets me into trouble.

I ran into the table last night.

I already have a BRUISE.

It hurts to touch the purple part.

It's something I'm happy to lose.

A BOOGER has a purpose.

It helps me breathe fresh air.

Dirt from the air gets trapped in the snot,

and forms a booger in there.

My cut dried into a SCAB.
It's hard and protects the cut.
Underneath it my body works,
to heal the whole thing up.

When I play in the hot Summer sun,
SWEAT makes my face really shiny.
I know that I need to drink a lot,
to put water back inside me.

*Most of the things I eat and drink,
my body uses for energy.
Everything it can not use,
comes out of my body as PEE.*

If I don't clean my EARWAX out,
It gets very hard to hear.
That's why Mom always keeps,
a box of cotton swabs near.

One time a bug flew into my eye,
and I was very surprised.
Even though I wasn't crying,
the TEARS were cleaning my eyes.

I scraped my knee and forgot to clean it.

I didn't keep it protected.

PUS started oozing out of it,

because it got infected.

PHLEGM is snot inside my throat.

Coughing helps clear it out.

It's yellow and really slimy,

so I always cover my mouth.

Last Winter I caught the flu,
and I got very sick.
I had to VOMIT into a bowl,
because I couldn't move very quick.

I have BLISTERS on my hands,
from holding my baseball bat.
They're little cushions filled with water.
When they pop, they go splat.

There's always SALIVA in my mouth.
It helps me swallow my food.
I only spit when brushing my teeth,
because Mom says spitting is rude.

Everybody has to POOP.
I go before I have a problem.
If I hold it in too long,
it can really hurt my bottom.

In the bath I wash everywhere,
especially between my toes,
because in those little spaces,
is where the TOE JAM grows.

When I FART really loud,
my Mom is never happy.
I shouldn't fart around other people,
or at least do it quietly.

My body is really funny.
Every day is something new.
Sometimes gross or scary,
and always right on cue.

All of it is normal.
I never need to shout!
Fluids, solids and gasses,
will always be coming out.

A BULLETPROOF TODDLER PUBLICATION

Made in the USA
Lexington, KY
17 December 2010